FINISHING LINE PRESS

www.finishinglinepress.com

The Body of All Things

poems by

Rebecca Jamieson

Finishing Line Press
Georgetown, Kentucky

The Body of All Things

ACKNOWLEDGMENTS

I would like to thank the following journals for their publication of individual
poems in previous versions:

AndReview: "Driftless," and "Away on the Wind"
Calyx: "Perseid"
M Review: "All the Spring Nights," "The Taste of Apple," and "Voices"
VoiceCatcher: "Cows"

Publisher: Leah Maines

Editor: Christen Kincaid

Cover Art: Aremy Stewart

Author Photo: Rebecca Jamieson

Cover Design: Elizabeth Maines McCleavy

Printed in the USA on acid-free paper.
Order online: www.finishinglinepress.com
            also available on amazon.com

Author inquiries and mail orders:
Finishing Line Press
P. O. Box 1626
Georgetown, Kentucky 40324
U. S. A.

Table of Contents

*To my family—those connected to me by blood,
and those by spirit. And to the aspiration that humans
may awaken to the heartfelt understanding that all beings
belong to the same family and the same body.*

Driftless

I.

At home
the heart wanders off.
The heart does not stay
in the cornfield at dusk
with birds black against red sky.
The heart does not stay
in the well my father
climbed down into weekly
his voice echoing up,
or in the black dirt of the garden
beneath my mother's hands.

II.

We don't speak
of this now.
When I was five
the only thing I feared
were ghosts.
I sang to them as I climbed
the blue stairs to the attic.
I offered them
my wakefulness
faking rigor mortis
to stave off death.

III.

When I was eighteen
I stood gazing through
white curtains.
In summer I felt the heat
move palpable as a hand
across my face,

seep down to my stomach.
I felt it every time
the red car drove past
spitting gravel,
one muscled arm hanging
from the window.
I forgot how to climb the apple tree.
I forgot what morning is.
I forgot the songs of grass.

IV.

What lies we tell
ourselves
wash out like blood,
go back to nourish
the earth we came from.
Was I trapped
underneath a bushel basket,
inside a mason jar,
stuck in the screws and mash
of the cider press?
Or was I just a visitor
left with the taste
of snow, mud, corn and apples,
the reeling line caught
in my lip.

Ghosts

I always squinted in childhood photographs, seeing what wasn't there. Voices woke me from sleep, asking questions I couldn't answer. In the morning, the garden was misty, forest-tall. I peered into tree knot-holes, whispering to the insects buried in wood, pressed my ear to the ground, listening for a heartbeat.

In the afternoons, my mother and I climbed Cemetery Hill. No one else was there, yet fresh plastic flowers always swayed in the wind. I wandered through the gravestones, carefully slid crayons over paper and stone. I made rubbings of angels and vines, small hands holding envelopes and violets. I couched by the worn-down nubbins of baby graves. Jane—two months, Alice—four years, Unnamed—three days. The sun slid into late afternoon, the sigh of August in the top of every tree.

When the light became low and golden, sadness overwhelmed me. I screamed hot-faced on the way home, understanding that my days were numbered. The ghosts had all the time in the world.

Knowing

I was the kid who always won the guessing
games at birthday parties, leaving
friends freckled and blank,
fists soft and half-melted around
pink napkins, chocolate whispering
above lips about to give
the wrong answer.

Mothers stopped letting me play.
There was nothing they could pull
from a paper bag I hadn't already seen,
no item small enough to hide
behind the dark corners of their ears.

I heard the numbers' square feet
marching whole minutes off,
saw them in a holy flash,
spit them out before I had time
to question how I knew.

They burned on my tongue
sweet as lightning.

A Complicated Plant

When I was a girl, nettles overtook
the garden. Wandering off the path

they towered over me, left pink, stinging
welts on my skin. My mother was busy elsewhere—

the nasturtiums were thirsty, aphids devoured
the kale with their translucent bodies.

No one knew what ailed me, why I screamed
for hours on the kitchen floor. No one dug below

the roots. A family is a complicated
plant. Which parts do we dry out in daylight?

Which parts do we leave buried?
Now I boil nettles, mash them

in my teeth. Now I value the bitter
medicines, the spiky plants

with poison flowers. Even a weed
has its purpose.

Family Land

We went to Family Land every summer, our family's one stab at being normal. My mother plastered sandwiches with mayonnaise and lunch meat, holding her lips tightly so as not to let slip the factory farm dirges held just behind her teeth. My father hummed under his breath, ignoring us as we drove through corn fields that touched the August sky. He would not shout this time. My swimsuit was handmade that year—black flowers with white trim. My long hair baked in two frizzy braids down my back. I was plump and tall and used words like surreptitious.

I refused to go down the big water slides—ones that sucked you into their blackness like holes inside a washing machine. I wore an orange nose-plug and plastic floaties, went down the kiddie water slides that ended in three feet of blueish chlorine. A boy screamed, "What are you, a baby?" and small, tan girls in pink and lavender bikinis streamed past me like schools of gum-chewing fish. The sun blistered my skin the color of its own scarlet face.

Watching my parents shimmer across the baking concrete, it was suddenly clear to me: one day I would have to step out past the rocking chair, past the piano and flower garden, into the world of TVs, freeways and cruelty. We bought tickets for the haunted coal mine, desperate to escape the sickly yellow heat. We sat in the rickety cart and I took my mother's hand. Then the curtains parted and we jostled off into the dark unknown.

Perseid

In the lonesome nights of August
my father and I lay in the middle
of the road, the sun's fierce
warmth embedded in blacktop, its radiance
lingering on the moon's wistful face.

Galaxies jittered above
rustling constellations of cornfields.
My father was quiet, arms crossed
over plaid workshirt, silvery head
a fallen star.

Clumps of fiery rock plummeted
toward us like lit matchbooks.
I heard them hiss and sputter
on the wet grass, silently
made wish after wish:
please let my father
see me.

I listened
to the wind move through
the corn, the space between
us, tried to absorb the distant
brilliant light.

The Taste of Apple

I was always afraid to climb trees. I wasn't scrappy or athletic like the other kids. When I was twelve, my body morphed into something unrecognizable, and I was seized with a desire for vantage, escape. I paced around the old apple tree, placed one hand on its blighted bark. I put my foot in the crotch, grabbed the limbs and pulled myself up. I inched farther up the branch, then farther still. The road opened itself below me, cornfields on both sides, one gray silo on the horizon. A motor grumbled in the distance, growing louder. A red Firebird appeared, one golden arm visible, one pale half-moon of face. I never saw the rest of the boy. I didn't need to. After that, I climbed the apple tree every day.

Cows

The black and white Holsteins
aren't tame.
They live on the other
side of the electric
fence, rolling their white eyes
if I get too close.

They smell of shit
grass and saliva
                    summer
            sweet hay
and the big night
sky, prickling
with stars.

They are in their own world—
fervent chewing
the twice daily mechanical milker.
I am in mine—
no friends, braces on my teeth
road that vanishes into corn fields.

I stand next to the fence
listen to its eager
hum, touch a grass blade
to it, just for the jolt
along my hand, the sudden
galloping of cows away
from such desperate
electricity.

Allegiance

Good morning sun, yellow
ball of fire in the sky.
Good morning misty city:
metal, glass and smoke.

Good morning to the thin
warbles of birds. Every year
there are fewer.

Constant rumble and whine
of traffic could be from one
of three freeways. What
did it sound like before?

Hopelessness comes
like an old dead end,
a metal trap. It is half-blind
always waiting.

The garden unfurls
robust kale, pungent oregano, awakened
orange chrysanthemums.

A crow breaks the blue air
with its harsh voice.
Two sparrows flap
determinedly. There are the choices
we make and the choices
we are given.

I choose allegiance
to the few and scattered voices
of the birds. I choose allegiance
to the kale and chrysanthemums
the imperfect unfurling
within all of us.

To the goodness
that hides in the smallest
of things.

Time Tunnels

I am living all moments of my life at once. The trapped, leathery feeling of the family car trip when I was seven: Dad exploding at a rest stop, shoulders huge in his plaid shirt, the landscape shocked in snow. That whiteness still leaps at me without warning, clutching my chest. When a man looks at me blankly, anger freezing his jawbone, there is that same shakiness, that blinding flash. When I am in the backseat of a car going much too fast.

I am foraging in the dark soil of the future as well. I run my fingers through its pebbles, encounter a familiar root or vine. Sometimes I write the date a year ahead. Do I exist there? They say *death comes without warning*, but just before the deer leaps into my headlights, I slow.

The future appears for a moment, but is never solid—a minnow between my fingers. It is always just *now*. If there is a future, I will be worrying there too, so busy tunneling into time I don't notice that I have already arrived.

Away on the Wind

We biked all day
escaping Portland.
The Willamette River kept track of us
past Swan Island, Ross Island, Toe Island.
The old amusement park watched
us wistfully, singing a tinny song
that blew away on the wind.

We time traveled
through small Midwestern towns
bright banners flying
antique stores mumbling the past.
Here is that mainstreet
you walked down once
on a yellow day in your childhood.
And here is the library
where I hid until closing time
reading *Jane Eyre.*

The towns that kept us safe once
dissolve as the sun sets, and we become
uncertain strangers beside each other
our breath mingling
with the wind from the river.
The stars come out as we return
to our new city.
I wonder if I can ever
go home again.

Labor

The bed is crumpled, deep, inviting. I heave off blankets, reveal white flannel sheets with faint, mysterious stain. I cover it quickly.

First I throw on the small quilt my mother, sister and I made. Some days I run my finger over the blue flower I embroidered in satin stitch when I was seven. Other days I get past it as quickly as possible. Hidden memories, sweet-bitter, raveled pieces of red and blue yarn holding the whole thing together. Coming undone bit by bit the older I get, the more I remember.

Next I smooth on the quilt bought from a yard sale. It should be on the bed of someone who knows its story, feels the love of the maker sink into their bones every night. But maybe they no longer wanted those lingering hands over their body in the dark liquid hours when the mind is most vulnerable.

Last I place the comforter: cheery red and blue geometric windmills on a white background. This one is for the guests, for people who want to peep in and say *oh what a pretty room.* This is the one I touch as I listen to the whine of cars from the street, examining my labor, waiting for my life to end or begin.

How to Avoid Change

Stick wool in your ears.
Close your eyes and refuse
to open them for anyone, even if he is trying
to show you something beautiful—a watercolor
pigment still wet and earthy
a bird skimming the silver grass of a field.

Hold onto things tightly.
Any large, immobile object will do:
dish-washers, monkey bars, trucks
porch railings, boulders.
Don't hang onto people.
People are always disappearing
just like ghosts.
They can only be counted on
to haunt you.

Close your mouth.
Change hovers just behind the teeth
ready to leap out.

Stay in the same town you grew up in
or pick the town you lived in the longest
and move back there.
You don't need to be happy
you will be safe.
You will recognize everything
with a sharp, defeated familiarity.

This morning the sky was pure gold
with one orange streak. Tonight
it is deep blue with thin pink threads.

Imagine you are a potted plant
a wreath made of dry twigs
an immaculate stainless steel surface
the placid curve of a mixing bowl.
Imagine you are a fresh white envelope
never sent.

The Body

A house that burns down so slowly nobody notices.

How Easily

I come upon a squirrel carcass
twisted in damp grass

beneath a sheltering oak, no longer
an animal, becoming
something else entirely:
birchbark, driftwood, honeycomb.

Its gnarled feet point up
the roots beneath point down.

I stand pointing straight
toward nightfall.

How easily I forget
that I could not be here at all.

Winter

Dead stalks
of Queen Anne's Lace
stand tall behind
abandoned house.

Frost nestles their roots
sky a cold
and empty blue.

A lumpy rind of moon
looks down
with one eye.

One small black bird
without wings
sits on the telephone wire

then
vanishes.

Isn't it Remarkable

That tonight I am a river of flame. That tomorrow all the raindrops falling will have soaked into the ground. That in a thousand years, the only ones to tell our stories will be the rocks. That in this furrowed darkness, I could reach out and take your hand.

I hold it

like an impossibly
delicate wine glass, impaled
with doubt, knowing
it will break.

But wine glasses are meant
for breaking.
      They yearn
            for it.

So drink darling
drink. Sip
if you have to, but
let it
       w   i   d   e   n
you —

the beauty
and the terror.

Licking the Buds

Western Red Cedar, California Bay
       Yellow Magnolia stretch green shoulders
under fine silver drizzle, breathe

damply, reach muscular roots
through dark stories of silt
and loam, branches embracing

the fine gray silk
of sky, creating
       a nest that holds me
above
       and below.

A bush unfurls
       an inch from my cheek
sticky green leaves
forming sharp, exquisite points

poised on the cusp
of spring.   A single drop
of rainwater hangs
reflecting my face
       upside down.

I lean in.

My tongue quivers
against the rough green skin
       for a moment
blood and sap
clamoring through veins.

Who am I
not to revel in this wild blossoming
       body
which is the body
       of all things.

All the Spring Nights

The air is thick, inhaling
I flush. Musk and root, crotch
and vine, stamen, pistil
sweaty sheets. Petals
envelop me: a cloud
of small, white tongues.

Last night I wore
a crown of antlers.
Your freckles tasted
like copper. Your skin smelled
of wood smoke, crocus.

I pressed against you
so slowly
you didn't wake
until I was wild
half-gone, hands turned hooves
black and cloven.

We are newly plowed
earth—that smell of iron
soft grasping
of ankles. We are
the ferocious darkness
that gives birth to the world.

Come to me tonight
and all the spring nights.
I am gibbous
silvery and full
of my own light.

Velocity

Remember when we were enlightened and grandiose and thought we could become whatever we wanted naturally as ice cream melting on our tongues and we were so sure it would happen that we didn't even try? Remember being twenty-three years old, living at an artists' residency in Vermont, sharing a haunted house that creaked and laughed at night in the voices of small girls? Remember the snow piled taller than our heads in places but it just kept snowing? Remember how I didn't know how to be a writer and you didn't know how to be an artist but we tried anyway, you with sawhorses and postage stamps, me with papers taped on my walls, humiliated by all the real writers with MFAs who acted like Raymond Carver was their best friend? Remember how I had a boyfriend back home but we fell in love anyway—deeper than the drifting snow or the icy Gihon river? There was no stopping it, no stopping us, and we learned to try with each other, to take nothing for granted, slowly realizing that there was so much we couldn't do, couldn't be with each other, but that somehow, we could find a way to be perfectly ourselves.

Eucalyptus

That burnt summer
in California

we went to an old
saloon, abandoned

between the prairie
and the sea.

All I remember
is the cutting light

the sun and dark
wooden hollows inside

people shot or hanged
or simply disappeared

from the weight
of their own solitude.

I saw you framed
in the doorway of blackened

timber and didn't recognize
your face. Outside

the Eucalyptus fluttered
thousands of tiny hands

blinding me with their silvery
light.

David

Sarah stands in the Uffizi
cool and still. Outside
July swelters the *piazza*, gilds
tourists, pickpockets, lovers
with the kind of golden light
Michelangelo painted.

We've been here an hour.
I want a strawberry gelato,
the sunburned air, an afternoon
glass of wine. I want to know
my older sister, the one
I have traveled halfway
around the world hoping
to find.

She is facing David
her blonde head small beneath
his magnificent toes.
She stands unmoving
amidst the pushing crowd.
A circle of light
surrounds them.

She doesn't see me.
She doesn't see anything
but what she has always wanted
to see: the perfection
of David's cold marble features,
the way his sightless eyes
look down on her with something
like love.

Voices

We are watching
you. Clouded, formless, we no longer have *I*

more than a drop of rain.
We are missing

legs, hair, teeth. We have been drowned, burnt
forgotten. We are missing

the broad, waxy leaves of summer beneath
fingers. Their secret trail on ankle, thigh...

We are missing a fragment—
the ricocheted sweetness of sparrow's song

reverberating in eardrums,
a steaming, bitter cup

of coffee, waiting
for a friend who never comes.

Our neighbors now are roots
and smoke. Fake flowers brittle
as wind passes through.

We feel your warmth, your busy little houses
beyond our gates. We listen to the incredible clockwork

of your hearts, envy your guts
their bubbling indiscretions, linger

next to your marvelous, silky
earlobes, drink down your ignorance—

a sweet bell that tolls on
and on.

Birds

In winter, the world was piled with white. A day could turn twilight then blink it was morning again. Curled by the woodstove, another twilight descended smoky, blue, so stealthy it barely made a sound.

I watched the birds at the feeder bolted outside the window, heaped with black sunflower seeds. Blue jay, chickadee, cardinal, nuthatch. Every once in a while, a downy woodpecker, its red head vivid against the snow.

Awaking from a dream where I floated just below the surface of an icy pond, a cardinal circling like a flame above my head, tapping the frozen surface with its beak, I rolled out of bed and bundled myself in coat, boots, hat, mittens. My mother was baking, my sister reading, my father at work. No one noticed as I opened the door, stepped outside.

The cold picked me up with both hands, roughed my cheeks, pulled my breath from me in smoky clouds. At the bird feeder, I leaned against the house, scooped seeds into my palm, extended my arm. Snow fell, thickening my lashes and running down my cheeks in tears. Hours passed, or minutes. I could have stood for days, breathing quietly, the snow covering my boots, reaching patiently for my ankles.

The birds watched me. Finally, a bold chickadee alighted with a whirl of wings on the tip of my mitten, weightless, fiercely gripping the wool. It gazed at me for a long while, then flew away, into the darkening trees and silently falling snow.

As You Were Meant to Be

Some yeses
come in a wild voice, others
are very quiet. Some call to you
from broken concrete
or the sweating noontime. Others

beckon you to the edge
of a field at nightfall, knowing
only that you must
place one timid foot
before the other.

Some yeses beg you
to stop—
encountering
a single orange poppy, heavy
with morning.

Still others whisper
that you should
                leap
your heels catching
at the unknown.

But all yeses—
the ones in yellow houses
and the ones in trees—
all call you down
into the deep, burning root
of yourself, out
into the true wide open
            asking you
to become as big
            as you were meant
                        to be.

Rebecca Jamieson grew up in the Driftless region of southwestern Wisconsin, and currently lives in Portland, Oregon, where she teaches writing and meditation. She holds an interdisciplinary BA from Marylhurst University in Writing, Mindfulness, and Psychology. Her publications include the *Shambhala Sun*, *Calyx*, *Stirring*, and *VoiceCatcher*. She has been awarded residencies at the Vermont Studio Center and the Spring Creek Project. In her free time, Rebecca volunteers as a facilitator with Write Around Portland, a nonprofit that offers writing workshops for those who wouldn't otherwise have access to writing and community.

CPSIA information can be obtained
at www.ICGtesting.com
Printed in the USA
LVOW11s0743280417
532494LV00001BA/33/P